W9-ASN-963

Pebble® Plus

ICE AGE ANIMALS

Woolly Mammoths

by Melissa Higgins

Consulting Editor: Gail Saunders-Smith, PhD

Content Consultant: Margaret M. Yacobucci, PhD
Education and Outreach Coordinator,
Paleontological Society; Associate Professor,
Department of Geology, Bowling Green State University

CAPSTONE PRESS
a capstone imprint

Pebble Plus is published by Capstone Press,
1710 Roe Crest Drive, North Mankato, Minnesota 56003
www.capstonepub.com

Library of Congress Cataloging-in-Publication Data
Higgins, Melissa, 1953– author.
Woolly Mammoths / by Melissa Higgins.
pages cm.—(Pebble Plus. Ice Age Animals)
Summary: "Describes the characteristics, food, habitat, behavior, and extinction of
woolly mammoths"—Provided by publisher.
Audience: Ages 5–7.
Audience: K to grade 3.
Includes bibliographical references and index.
ISBN 978-1-4914-2102-4 (library binding)
ISBN 978-1-4914-2320-2 (paperback)
ISBN 978-1-4914-2343-1 (ebook pdf)
1. Woolly mammoth—Juvenile literature. 2. Extinct mammals--Juvenile literature. I. Title.
QE882.P8H54 2015
569.67—dc23   2014028918

Editorial Credits
Jeni Wittrock, editor; Peggie Carley and Janet Kusmierski, designers;
Wanda Winch, media researcher; Laura Manthe, production specialist

Photo Credits
Illustrator: Jon Hughes
Shutterstock: Alex Staroseltsev, snowball, April Cat, icicles, Leigh Prather, ice crystals, LilKar, cover
background, pcruciatti, interior background

Note to Parents and Teachers

The Ice Age Animals set supports national science standards related to life science. This
book describes and illustrates woolly mammoths. The images support early readers in
understanding the text. The repetition of words and phrases helps early readers learn
new words. This book also introduces early readers to subject-specific vocabulary words,
which are defined in the Glossary section. Early readers may need assistance to read
some words and to use the Table of Contents, Glossary, Read More, Internet Sites, and
Index sections of the book.

Printed in China by Nordica.
0914/CA21401504
092014   008470NORDS15

Table of Contents

Ice-Age Giant

The ground shakes.

A 5-ton (4,540-kilogram)

woolly mammoth lumbers

over a hill. She leads

her herd to a green valley.

Mammoths lived during the
Ice Age. The climate was cool.
But there was plenty of grass.
Mammoths roamed grasslands
in Eurasia and North America.

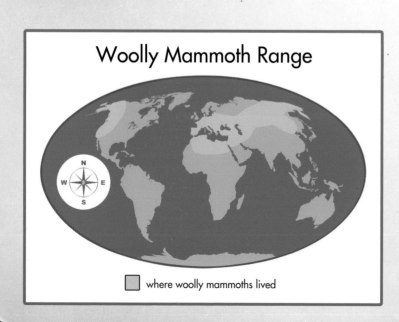

Woolly Mammoth Range

☐ where woolly mammoths lived

Built for Cold

A woolly mammoth was about the size of an elephant. But it was built for cold weather. Its small ears lost little heat. Long, shaggy fur kept it warm.

Tusks helped mammoths dig up food buried in snow. Mothers used tusks to protect calves from enemies. Males used tusks to battle each other.

Super Grazer

Mammoths used their trunks to eat and drink. They ate mostly grass. They needed 500 pounds (227 kilograms) of food every day.

Two "fingers" on the tip of the
mammoth's trunk plucked grass.
Bumpy ridges on their teeth
ground these tough plants.

Mammoth Life

Woolly mammoths lived in groups, like elephants today.

One female would lead a herd of other females and calves.

Adult males lived on their own.

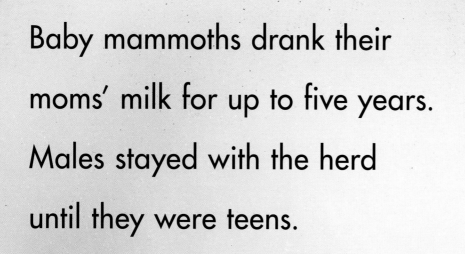

Baby mammoths drank their
moms' milk for up to five years.
Males stayed with the herd
until they were teens.

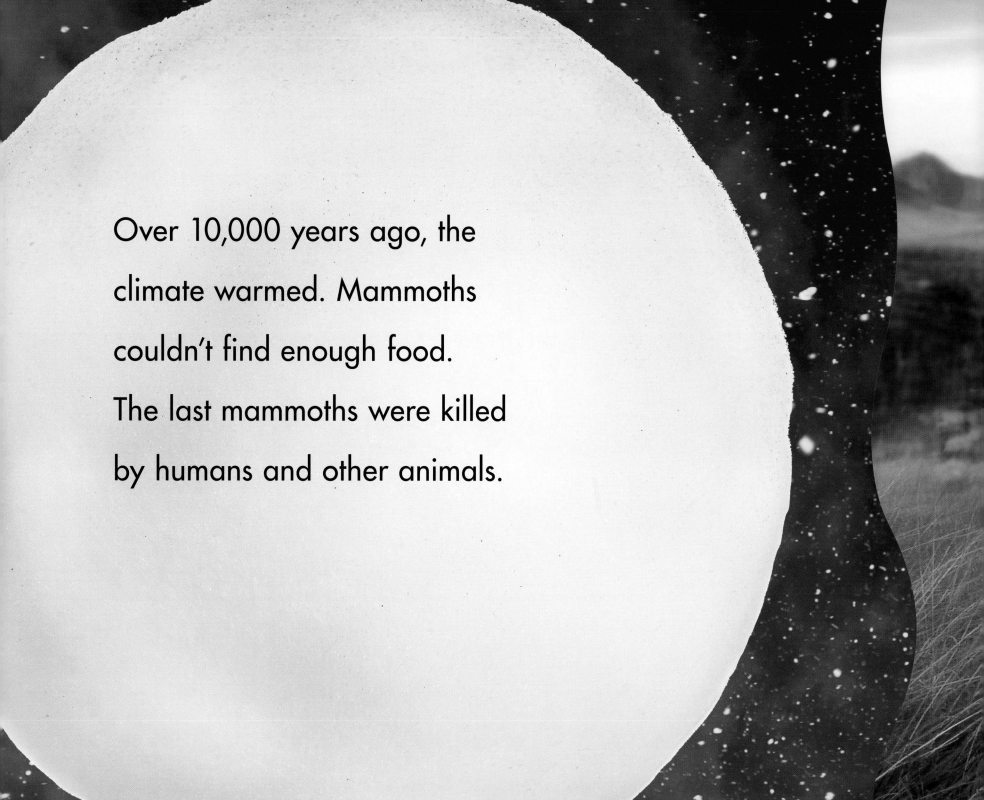

Over 10,000 years ago, the climate warmed. Mammoths couldn't find enough food. The last mammoths were killed by humans and other animals.

Glossary

calf—a baby woolly mammoth

climate—average weather of a place throughout the year

Eurasia—part of the world that includes Europe and Asia

grazer—an animal that eats grass

herd—a group of mammoths

Ice Age—a time when much of Earth was covered in ice; the last ice age ended about 11,500 years ago

lumber—to walk with slow, heavy steps

protect—to keep safe

shaggy—long and rough

trunk—a mammoth's long nose and upper lip

tusk—a long, pointed tooth that sticks out when the mouth is closed

Read More

Bailey, Gerry. *Woolly Mammoth.* Smithsonian Prehistoric Zone. New York: Crabtree, 2011.

Brown, Charlotte Lewis. *After the Dinosaurs.* I Can Read. New York: Harper Collins, 2011.

Manning, Mick and Brita Granstrom. *Woolly Mammoth.* London: Frances Lincoln Children's Books, 2011.

Internet Sites

FactHound offers a safe, fun way to find Internet sites related to this book. All of the sites on FactHound have been researched by our staff.

Here's all you do:

Visit *www.facthound.com*

Type in this code: 9781491421024

Check out projects, games and lots more at
www.capstonekids.com

Index

Word Count: 206
Grade: 1
Early-Intervention Level: 18